Dear Parent:

Congratulations! Your child is taking
the first steps on an exciting journey.
The destination? Independent reading!

STEP INTO READING® will help your child get there. The program offers
five steps to reading success. Each step includes fun stories and colorful art.
There are also Step into Reading Sticker Books, Step into Reading Math
Readers, Step into Reading Phonics Readers, Step into Reading Write-In
Readers, and Step into Reading Phonics Boxed Sets—a complete literacy
program with something to interest every child.

Learning to Read, Step by Step!

Ready to Read   Preschool–Kindergarten
• big type and easy words • rhyme and rhythm • picture clues
For children who know the alphabet and are eager to
begin reading.

Reading with Help   Preschool–Grade 1
• basic vocabulary • short sentences • simple stories
For children who recognize familiar words and sound out
new words with help.

Reading on Your Own   Grades 1–3
• engaging characters • easy-to-follow plots • popular topics
For children who are ready to read on their own.

Reading Paragraphs   Grades 2–3
• challenging vocabulary • short paragraphs • exciting stories
For newly independent readers who read simple sentences
with confidence.

Ready for Chapters   Grades 2–4
• chapters • longer paragraphs • full-color art
For children who want to take the plunge into chapter books
but still like colorful pictures.

STEP INTO READING® is designed to give every child a successful
reading experience. The grade levels are only guides. Children can progress
through the steps at their own speed, developing confidence in their
reading, no matter what their grade.

Remember, a lifetime love of reading starts with a single step!

Cover illustration is based on frame 353 of the Patterson-Gimlin film, copyright © 1967 by Martin and Erik Dahinden, with permission from Erik Dahinden.

Photographs: Page 15: Courtesy Humboldt State University Library, Special Collections; page 20: Stone head (21.8 cm. high) from The Dalles, Wasco County, Oregon, USA. YPM catalog no. ANT.003152. Photograph by William K Sacco. © 2004 Peabody Museum of Natural History, Yale University. All rights reserved; page 21: © President and Fellows of Harvard College, Peabody Museum of Archaeology and Ethnology, 14-7-10/85877; page 23: American Museum of Natural History/Denis Finnin; page 24: Topical Press Agency/Getty Images; page 25: Popperfoto/Getty Images; page 36: Photo by David R. Hunt, NMNH Phys. Antho. Cat # 390033, courtesy Dept. of Anthropology, Smithsonian Institution, Washington, DC; page 44: Fortean Picture Library.

Published in the United States by Random House Children's Books, a division of Random House, Inc., New York.

Visit us on the Web!
www.stepintoreading.com
www.randomhouse.com/kids

Educators and librarians, for a variety of teaching tools, visit us at
www.randomhouse.com/teachers

Library of Congress Cataloging-in-Publication Data
Worth, Bonnie.
Looking for Bigfoot / by Bonnie Worth ; illustrated by Jim Nelson. — 1st ed.
  p. cm. — (Step into reading)
ISBN 978-0-375-86331-8 (pbk.) — ISBN 978-0-375-96331-5 (lib. bdg.)
1. Sasquatch—Juvenile literature. I. Nelson, Jim, ill. II. Title.
QL89.2.S2 W68 2010
001.944—dc22
2009042727

Printed in the United States of America
10 9 8 7 6 5 4 3 2 1

LOOKING FOR BIGFOOT

by Bonnie Worth

illustrated by Jim Nelson

Random House 🏠 New York

Chapter One
SEEING IS BELIEVING

In the fall of 1869, a reporter for the
Antioch *Ledger* goes deer hunting in
the mountains, twenty miles south of
Grayson, California. When he returns to
his camp, he sees that someone has stirred
up his fire. He circles his camp and finds
large bare footprints in the dirt. Who—
or what?—has been messing with his
campsite?

He hides on a nearby hillside and waits
to find out.

Hours later, the hunter hears a high, eerie whistle that raises the hairs on his arms. Then he sees someone standing next to his fire. But this is no man! It has a long torso, short legs, and a small head with a flat nose and deep-set eyes. It is covered all over with hair, like an ape.

It whistles again and stoops to grab a burning stick from the fire. It swings the stick over its head, the embers streaking like fireworks. Soon it is joined by a second ape-like creature. The two of them walk off together, passing within twenty yards of the hunter, who cannot believe his eyes.

Now let's fast-forward to 2002. Helen Pahpasay and her mother go blueberry picking just north of Grassy Narrows, in Ontario, Canada. They are driving in their truck when they spot a hulking figure on the side of the road. It stands about eight feet tall, with an ape-like face, and is covered with long blackish red hair.

The ape-man ducks into the woods, but the women are too terrified to get out of the truck and follow it.

Later, the mother and daughter
tell reporters what they have seen.
Investigators who return to the site find
huge, sixteen-inch-long footprints in
the dirt.

When the report is aired on TV later that night, calls pour into the station. Many callers also claim to have seen giant footprints or huge, hairy ape-men lurking in those same woods.

Over the last two hundred years,
there have been more than two thousand
sightings of wild ape-men reported in
America. Most have been made in the
mountains and forests of the Northwest.

The sightings tend to sound very much alike. Eyewitnesses tell of a large, hairy, ape-like creature that stands on two legs. The creature is usually seen by itself, in the woods at night. Some people say they have heard it scream or whistle. Others have smelled something that makes them want to gag. Still others say that they have seen only its footprints. Some have made plaster casts of the footprints. Here is your proof, they say, that Bigfoot really exists.

But does Bigfoot really exist? Or is it only a myth?

Chapter Two
IT'S ALL A HOAX!

In 1958, Ray Wallace was a construction boss in Bluff Creek, in Northern California. He told of seeing huge footprints on his work site in the woods. Jerry Crew, a man who worked for him, traced one of the footprints on a piece of cardboard and took it to a local tracker. The tracker showed him how to take a plaster cast of it. Jerry Crew and his sixteen-inch plaster cast of a "big foot" appeared on the front page of the *Humboldt Times*. The mysterious track was dubbed Bigfoot, and the name stuck.

From the beginning, most people thought the footprint was a hoax. After all, Ray Wallace was known as a practical joker. "Why would I pull a hoax?" Ray said. "This thing is bad for business. Some of my men were so scared they quit."

But real or a hoax, the Bigfoot prints on Ray's work site got lots of people interested. They started to collect Bigfoot news stories and Bigfoot footprints. They formed Bigfoot clubs and went on Bigfoot scouting trips.

Gerald (Jerry) Crew measures his big foot.

Years later, Ray admitted to friends that it was all a hoax. Ray had made the footprints using big wooden feet tied to his shoes with leather straps. When Ray died, one newspaper claimed, "Bigfoot just died."

With hoaxes like Ray's, it's hard for most of us to know what to believe about Bigfoot. But scientists need more than eyewitness reports or plaster casts, which can easily be faked. They need strong, solid, scientific proof.

Chapter Three

THE WILD MAN
OF THE WOODS

Scientists believe that there are no apes native to North America, now or ever. So how could Bigfoot exist?

Scientists who study native cultures have always believed that there is a kernel of truth to be found in folklore and myths. People all over the world make up myths to explain things they don't understand, like how babies might go missing or how hunting camps get wrecked. Almost all tribes native to the Pacific Northwest tell the tale of a wild man living in the woods.

The Salish Indians of British Columbia called the mythical creature Sasquatch (SAS-quahtch), which means "wild man of the woods." The Hupa Indians of Northern California called it Oh-Mah, which means "boss of the woods." The Salish and the Hupa both believe in this ape-man, and they aren't the only ones.

The Tsimshian (CHIM-she-un) people have lived in the Pacific Northwest since before Columbus. They tell the tale of ba'oosh (bah-OOSH), which means "ape" or "monkey." Ancient carvings made from stones from the Columbia River show what some people consider the head of ba'oosh. It looks like that of an ape.

An ancient stone "monkey" head.

If there were no apes living nearby, if there were no TVs or magazines like there are today, how did the Tsimshian people know what apes looked like? And if there were apes in North America, how did they get there? And where are their bones or fossils? To answer these questions, we must first go to China.

Tsimshian mythical being mask.

Chapter Four

THE BIGFOOT-YETI-GIGANTO THEORY

In 1935, German scientist Ralph von Koenigswald began searching Chinese medicine shops for "dragon bones." Dr. von Koenigswald was a paleontologist, a person who studies fossils. He knew these dragon bones were really the teeth of ancient mammals. In Hong Kong, he found a gigantic tooth of an ape twice the size of a gorilla. The ape lived one million to 300,000 years ago. Dr. von Koenigswald named it *Gigantopithecus* (jie-gan-toh-PITH-ih-kus).

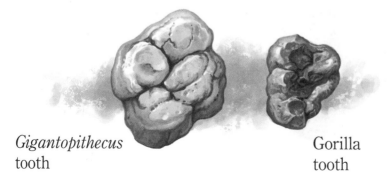

Gigantopithecus tooth

Gorilla tooth

In 1950, an Italian expedition to China found a fossil jawbone of this ancient ape. By studying the teeth and jawbone, scientists were able to figure out that *Gigantopithecus* probably looked something like a modern orangutan. And an orangutan looks something like a yeti (YEH-tee). What's that?

Gigantopithecus model from the American Museum of Natural History.

The yeti is an ape-man, somewhat like Bigfoot, sighted in the snow-capped mountains of Tibet. Reports go back hundreds of years. But people in the West didn't know much about the yeti until 1951. That year, on an expedition up Mount Everest, British mountaineer Eric Shipton photographed a line of huge footprints in the snow. The footprints were crisp, showing five toes.

Yeti footprint with ice ax head.

Shipton's photographs and stories were sent to newsrooms around the world. Suddenly everyone was talking about the yeti. They called him the Abominable Snowman. There were magazine articles, stuffed toys, and even a Hollywood movie.

Yeti footprints leading off into the mountains.

While lots of people had fun with the idea of the yeti, most people didn't really believe it existed. They said the footprints were made by a Tibetan blue bear and that the sun had melted them and made them appear bigger. Some said that the footprints belonged to a human hermit. Others said it was just a hoax.

But a few people believed the footprints were real. They also saw that the prints looked a lot like the Bigfoot footprints that had been found in North America. These people started thinking that both the yeti and Bigfoot were proof that *Gigantopithecus*, the ancient giant ape, still roamed the earth.

It is easier to believe that the yeti might be related to *Gigantopithecus*. After all, they are both from the same continent of Asia. But Bigfoot is in North America. How did it get all the way from Asia to North America? The answer is, perhaps, just the way mankind did: on foot.

Geologists believe that several times in prehistory, the continents of Asia and North America were connected by a land bridge that stretched from Siberia to Alaska. Bigfoot researchers believe that *Gigantopithecus* crossed the land bridge and traveled south to what is now the Pacific Northwest.

But like the woolly mammoth
and the saber-toothed tiger, wouldn't
Gigantopithecus be extinct by now? Not
necessarily. Some animals thought to be
long extinct have been discovered alive
and well.

In 1938, in East London, South Africa,
museum worker Marjorie Latimer found a
beautiful purple-blue fish on the deck of a
fishing boat owned by a friend.

She took the dead fish back to the museum with her in a taxi. There she looked in her books for a picture to match the fish. She could not believe what she was seeing. The fish on her desk matched the picture of a coelacanth (SEE-luh-canth), thought to have been extinct for over seventy million years!

If a "living fossil" like the coelacanth still swims the seas, why *can't* a giant ape still roam the woods of North America or the mountains of Tibet?

These are the kinds of questions cryptozoologists (krip-tuh-zoh-AHL-uh-jists) ask. Cryptozoologists are people who study animals that may or may not exist and are known only from eyewitness accounts. Cryptozoologists seek scientific proof that such "mythic" animals do, in fact, exist.

Some of these animals are rather small and dull, but others, like the Loch Ness monster and the kraken, are big and exciting. Cryptozoologists also hunt for proof that extinct animals, like *Gigantopithecus,* still survive in the form of Bigfoot or the yeti.

Cryptozoologists are often asked this question: If *Gigantopithecus* made its way to North America, why *haven't* any fossils been found?

Their usual answer is that only an armful of such fossils has been found in Asia. Fossils are rare even under the best of conditions. The damp climate of northwestern America is not ideal for preserving bones. Weather, decay, and wild animals make most old bones disappear.

If there are no remains to be found anywhere, where, then, is the scientific proof of the existence of Bigfoot?

Chapter Five

SCIENTIFIC PROOF?

There *is* some evidence to suggest that Bigfoot is real. Out of the hundreds of casts taken of footprints, some are clearer than others. A few even show the texture of the skin on the bottom of the foot. Modern apes have ridges on the soles of their feet. Dr. Grover Krantz found similar ridges in Bigfoot prints collected in southeastern Washington. At least one expert on fingerprints says these prints are real.

390033

Footprint cast made by Dr. Grover Krantz in 1982.
Inset shows close-up of skin ridges.

In addition to these ridged footprints, there is one other well-studied print. In 2000, Bigfoot researchers on an expedition to Washington's Skookum Meadows made an amazing discovery. They found a print of a creature that had reclined in the mud to reach some fruit they had left out overnight. The next morning, researchers used two hundred pounds of plaster to get not just a footprint but also casts of the heel, thigh, buttocks, and arm of the creature. There were also hairs taken from the site that tests later showed came from a primate.

People looking for Bigfoot have also used expensive recording equipment to catch sounds in the deep woods. High, eerie whistles and screams are hair-raising to hear.

Zoologists listening to these tapes have been unable to say that these sounds come from any known creature. Who made them, then? Maybe one Bigfoot calling out to another across the forest?

If there are foot, body, and voiceprints, why has no one ever found a body, either shot by a hunter or dead of natural causes? There is no good answer to this question other than that the woods are vast enough to hide a Bigfoot, dead or alive.

Why aren't there more photos? People don't always have their cameras handy when a Bigfoot walks across their path. Many witnesses have also reported that they were too scared or too astonished to reach for their cameras in time.

There might not be many photos, but there is a short film that Bigfoot believers think offers up the most powerful proof of all.

Chapter Six

LIGHTS, CAMERA, ACTION—BIGFOOT!

One day in October 1967, two men set out on horseback into the wilds of Bluff Creek, California. Their names are Roger Patterson and Bob Gimlin. They aim to find a Bigfoot and to capture it on film.

After a few days of searching, they come to a stream where their horses begin to snort and shy. What are they afraid of? One of the horses rears and throws Gimlin. Suddenly both men see what has spooked the horses. Directly across the stream stands a real, live Bigfoot!

While his horse wheels in panic, Patterson grabs his camera from his saddlebag and starts filming. The Bigfoot looks like a female because it has breasts. She pauses and turns to look into the camera. Then she walks upstream and straight into the brush.

Frame 352 of the Patterson film.

Even though this is what the men have come for, they are still amazed that they actually found a Bigfoot. After they calm their horses, Roger and Bob take plaster casts of the footprints the creature has left in the soft, damp sand by the stream.

Scientists from all over the world have pored over this one short film. Some say it is just a hoax. It's a man in a gorilla suit, they say. Others say it is real. How else can you explain the muscles rippling beneath the fur?

A Hollywood special-effects man who is an expert in gorilla suits looks at the film. He swears that it can't *possibly* be a costume. The people at Disney Pictures say the film would be nearly impossible to fake. Even Dian Fossey, world-famous expert on gorillas, says on TV that she believes that the Patterson film, along with other evidence, calls for a major scientific study of the giant ape-man.

Perhaps someday, one of the many scientific expeditions now scouring the forests of the Great Northwest will dig up some bones or fossils, or maybe even come face to face with a living, breathing Bigfoot.

Until that day comes, we will keep our minds open and our eyes on the deep woods. And we will wonder. . . .